Book 2 - Moving on

'Play your Ocarina' Book 2 First published 1992 **ISBN 1 871210 05 4**
'Play your Ocarina' Book 2 CD edition First published 2006 **ISBN 1 871210 26 7**

All contents and musical arrangements copyright © 1992 David and Christa Liggins,
Ocarina Workshop, PO Box 56, Kettering, NN15 5LX, UK.

**All rights reserved.
Please remember photocopying music is illegal and unfair.**

No part of this publication may be reproduced, stored in a retrieval system, or transmitted
in any form or by any means, electronic, mechanical, photocopying, recording or otherwise,
without prior permission in writing from Ocarina Workshop at the address above.

Contents

Moving on	3	The cuckoo	19
Greensleeves	4	Sing a little song	20
Home on the range	6	Tallis' canon	21
Barges	8	Muss i'denn	22
Gypsy rover	10	Nose-shading	24
Cockles and mussles	12	Skip to my Lou	24
Music for marching and dancing	13	National anthem	25
Le maître de la maison	13	Thumb-holes	26
Floral dance	14	Auld lang syne	27
Shepherd's hey	15	Semitones	28
Can Can	16	Black eyes	28
Wedding marches	17	Spring song	29
Group and part playing	18	My grandfather's clock	30
Chopsticks	18	For he's a jolly good fellow	32

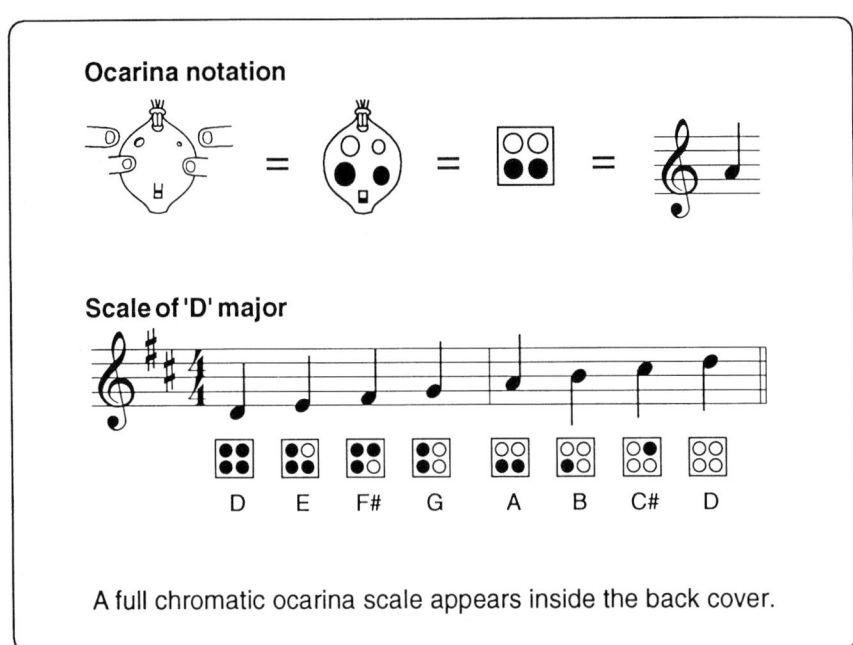

A full chromatic ocarina scale appears inside the back cover.

Moving on

In book 1 of this series, 'Starting off', we introduced the basics of playing the ocarina. In the first section of book 2, 'Moving on', we introduce song and dance tunes from around the world to widen your horizons. If you think your tonguing and slurring are going well, see how quickly you can attack the 'Can Can' or how beautifully you are able to phrase 'Greensleeves'.

Can you produce a full enough sound for the 'Wedding march'? Will your performance of it be likened to that of a grand cathedral organ or a wheezy old harmonium? Only you can answer these questions - or those who are within earshot! Hide away and practise those long notes and tonguing exercises we recommended in book 1 and you will soon be ready to try the trickiest tunes in the book.

In the second half of 'Moving on' we introduce part playing. Ocarina players don't all come in twos and threes so we've chosen material that will also make attractive solos. However, adding optional harmonies here and on every page in book 3 means that some may play duets instead of solos and even start their own groups.

Both books 3 and 4 also assume that you can play all the notes inside the back cover. Some of these notes take some practice and so this book introduces such wonderfully unique skills as 'nose-shading', 'thumb-waggling' and 'half-covering' to help you reach a pinnacle of skilled performance. Once mastered you will find endless enjoyment in effortlessly gliding through the contents of this book and on through the most demanding solos we can throw at you in book 4.

Most of all we hope that you will enjoy 'Moving on'. May each page be a delight to you and those you entertain. Breathe life into your ocarina and into each page as it opens.

Remember:

- Keep your ocarina safely in its box or round your neck
- If others play your ocarina, sterilise it in a sterilising fluid
- When playing, tilt the string-end towards the ground
- Place your third and fourth fingers on the string-hole to support your oc
- Experiment with the strength of your breath to produce a good tone

Greensleeves

16th century English

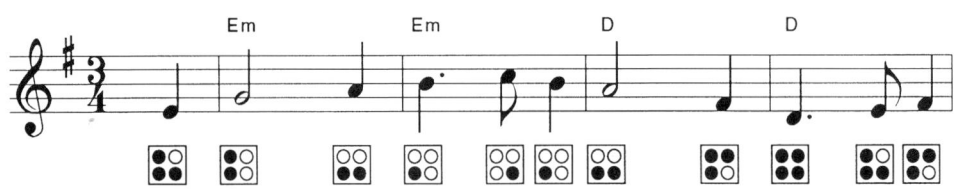
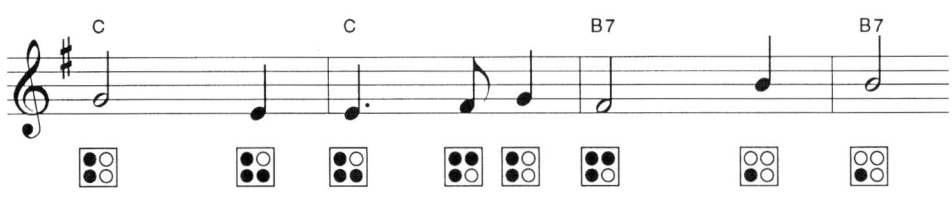
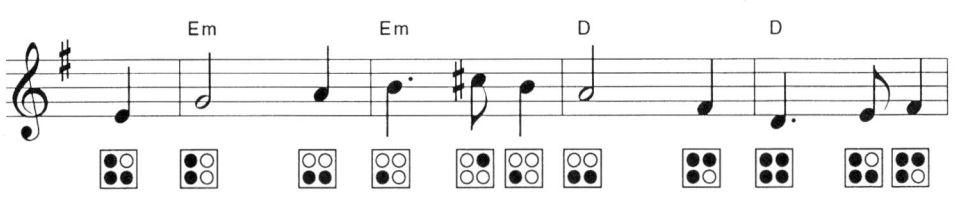
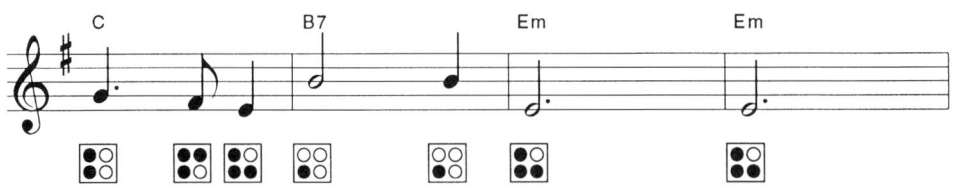

'Greensleeves' was a well known tune in Shakespeare's day and is mentioned in his play 'The Merry Wives of Windsor'. It has been adapted here for the ocarina.

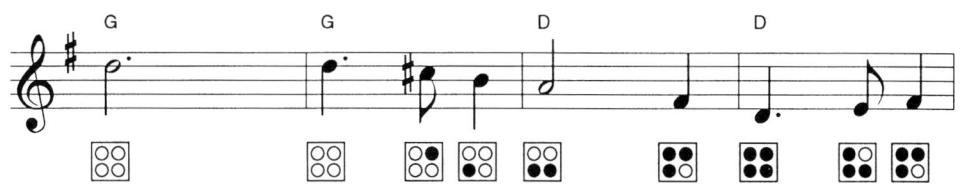
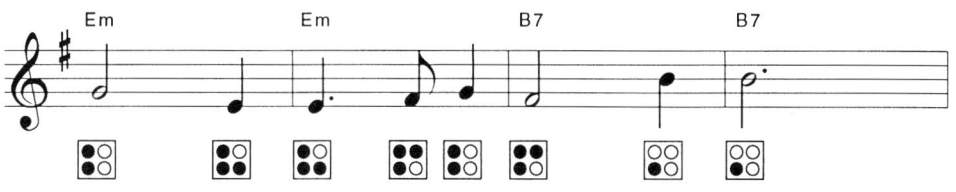
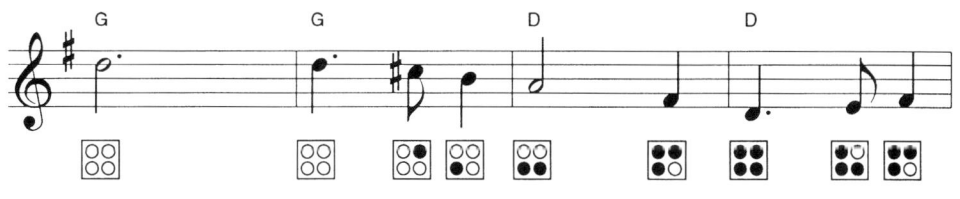
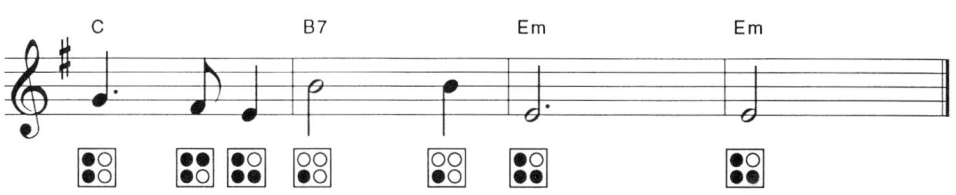

Home on the range

Cowboy song

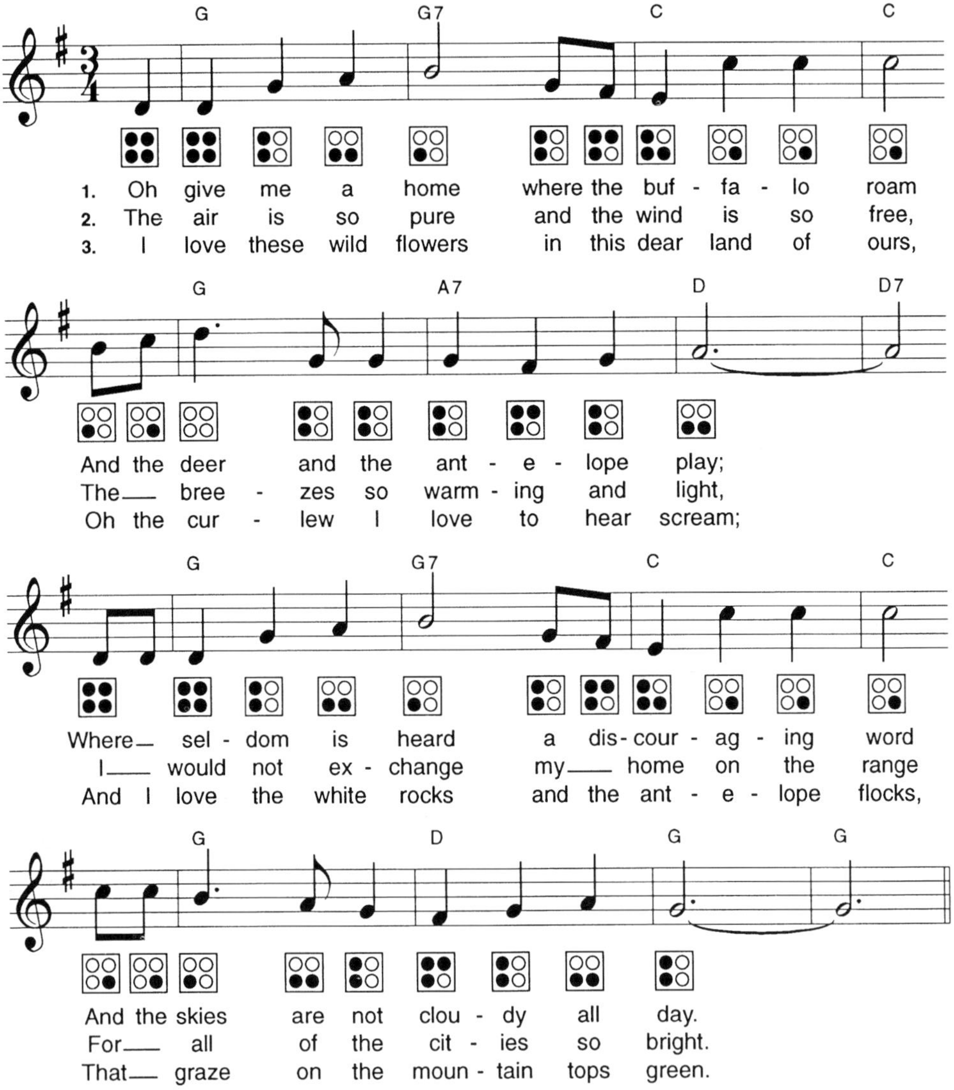

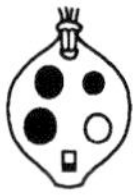

Barges

Dutch song

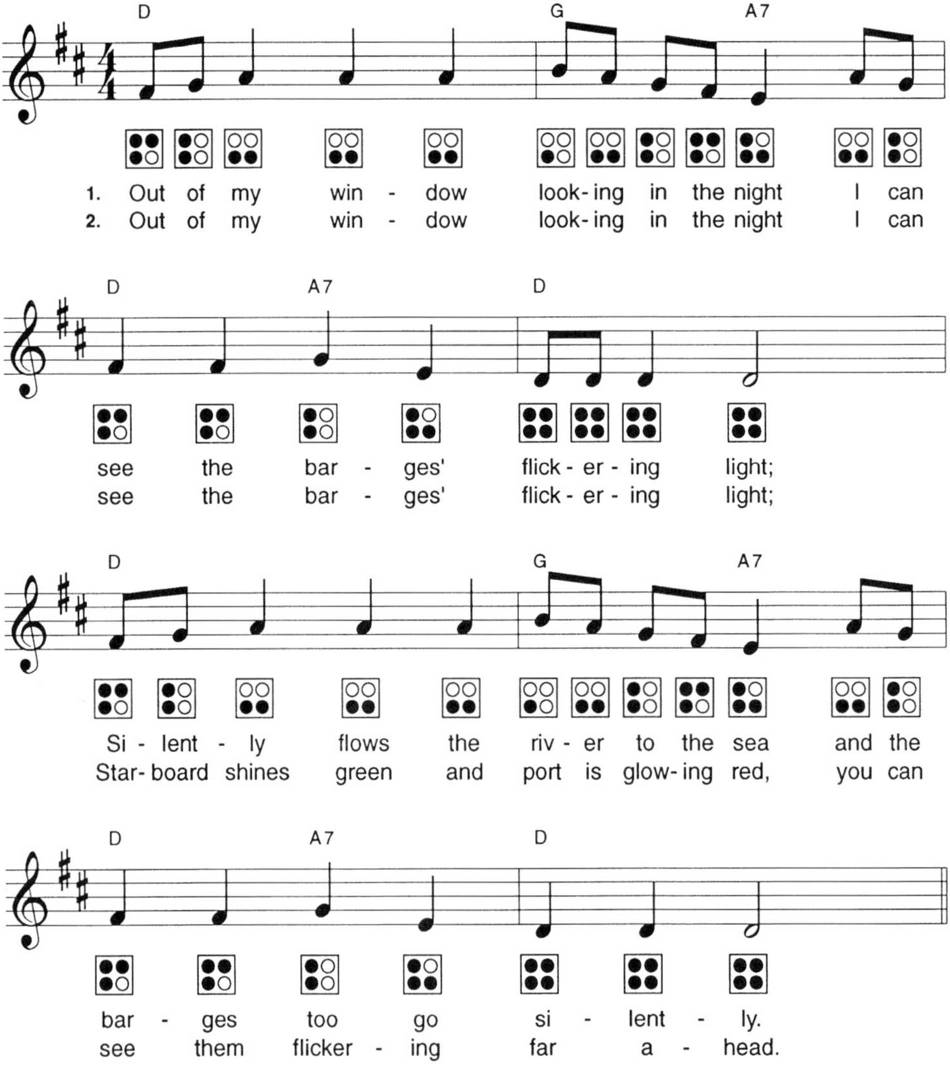
D G A7
1. Out of my win - dow look-ing in the night I can
2. Out of my win - dow look-ing in the night I can
D A7 D
see the bar - ges' flick - er - ing light;
see the bar - ges' flick - er - ing light;
D G A7
Si - lent - ly flows the riv - er to the sea and the
Star-board shines green and port is glow-ing red, you can
D A7 D
bar - ges too go si - lent - ly.
see them flicker - ing far a - head.

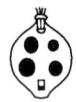

Gypsy rover

Irish traditional

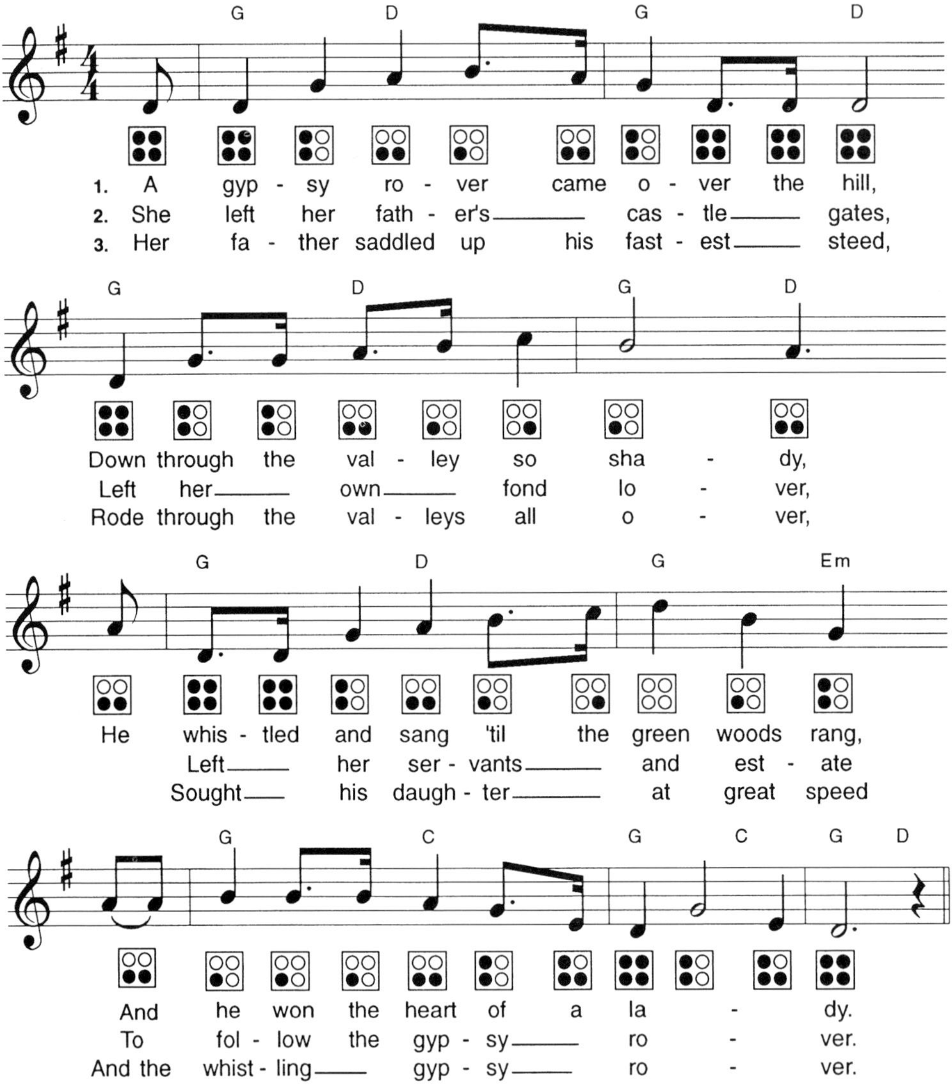
G D G D
1. A gyp - sy ro - ver came o - ver the hill,
2. She left her fath - er's cas - tle gates,
3. Her fa - ther saddled up his fast - est steed,
G D G D
Down through the val - ley so sha - dy,
Left her own fond lo - ver,
Rode through the val - leys all o - ver,
G D G Em
He whis - tled and sang 'til the green woods rang,
Left her ser - vants and est - ate
Sought his daugh - ter at great speed
G C G C G D
And he won the heart of a la - dy.
To fol - low the gyp - sy ro - ver.
And the whist - ling gyp - sy ro - ver.

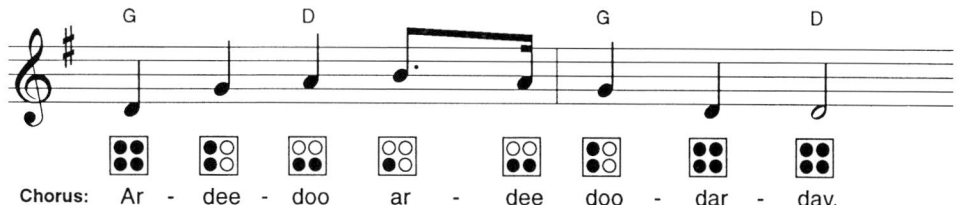
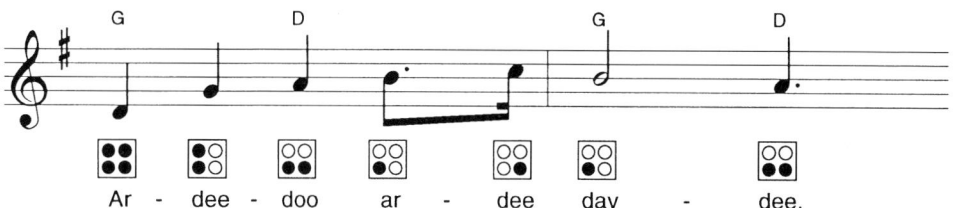
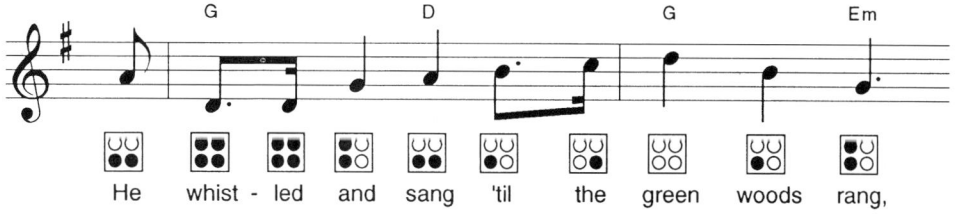
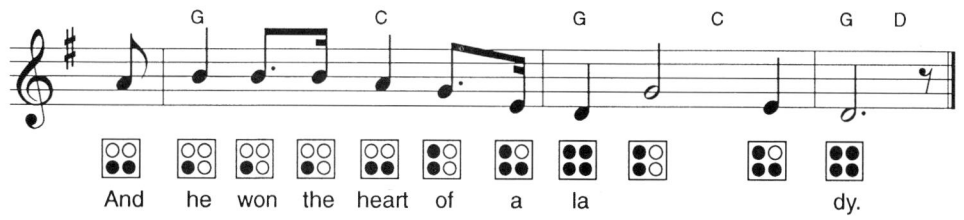

4. He came at last to a mansion fine,
   Down by the River Plady,
   And there was music and there was wine
   For the gypsy and his lady.

5. "He is no gypsy, my father' she said
   "But lord of these lands all over,
   And I will stay 'til my dying day
   With my whistling gypsy rover".

Cockles and mussels
Irish song

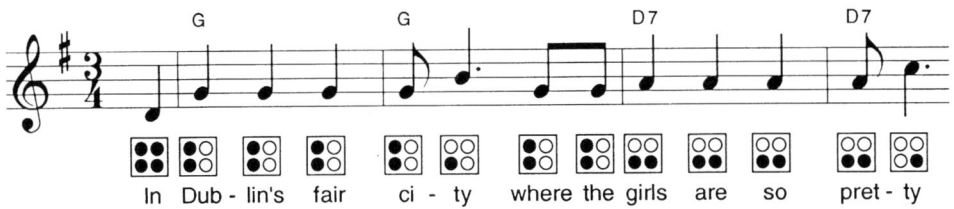

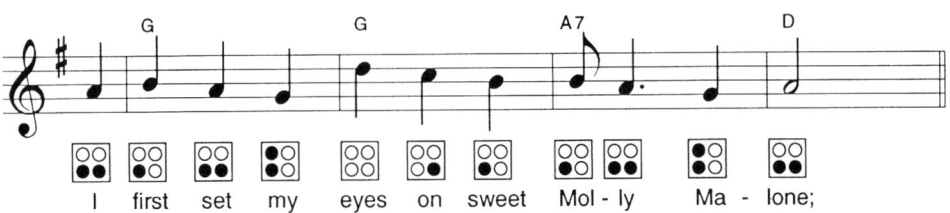

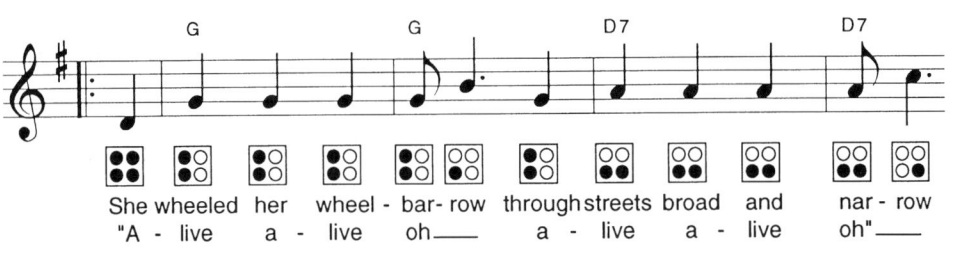

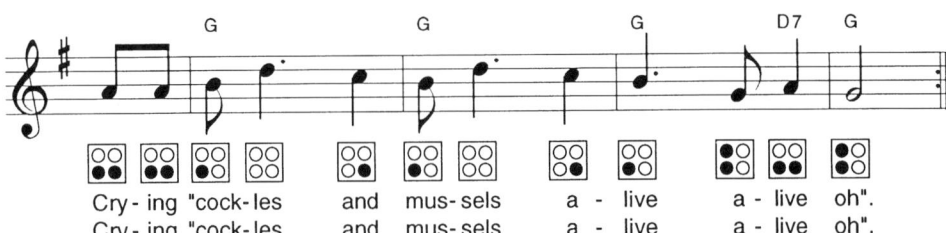

Double bars at the beginning and end of the last section have dots added. These tell you to repeat everything in that section. See more repeat signs in the tune opposite.

Music for marching and dancing

Music is traditionally played at many occasions ranging from great ceremonial events to the local village 'hop'. The music in this section includes wedding marches, normally associated with the thunderous sound of the church organ, through to morris dance tunes played traditionally on pipe and tabor.

Play morris dance and processional tunes with a steady rhythm. The Can Can and the tune below can speed up as fast as you are able to play or dance them.

A new dance is introduced below with words describing the steps. It is possible to play and dance at the same time. Stand in a circle, joining hands if possible, and walk two steps to the left, then two steps to the right. Repeat. Then take one step left and one step right. Repeat. Finally, let go of hands, turn clockwise around on the spot and join hands to immediately start playing and dancing again.

 ## Le maître de la maison *French dance*

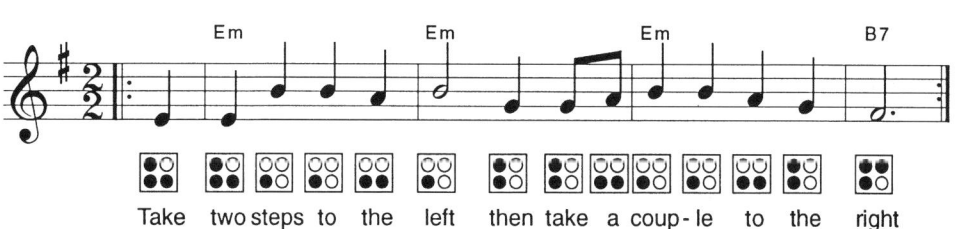

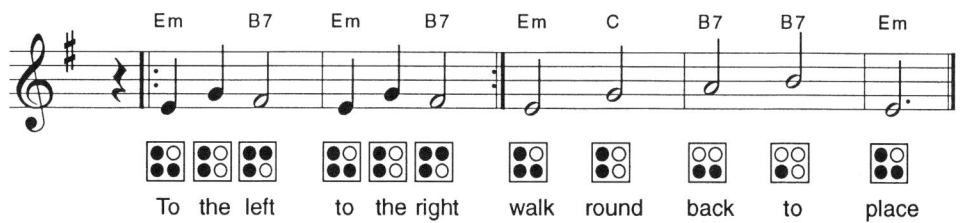

book 2   arrangement copyright © 1992 Ocarina Workshop Publications - copying prohibited

Floral dance

Cornish

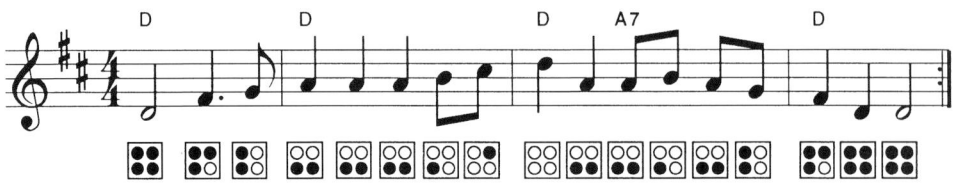
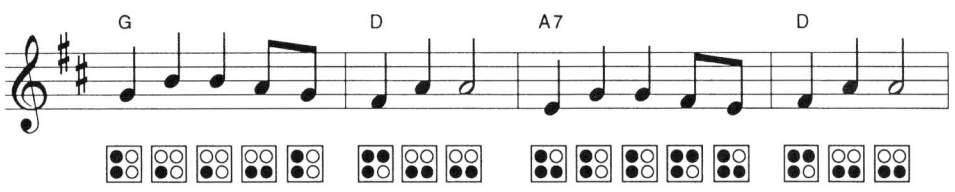
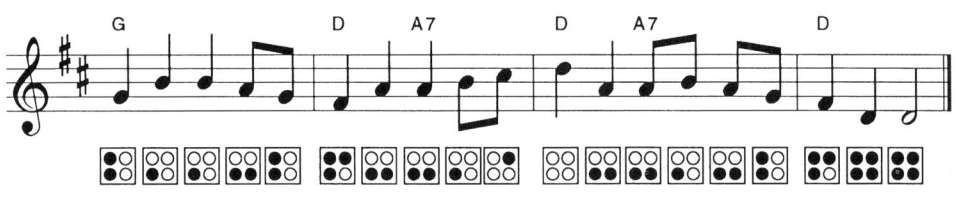
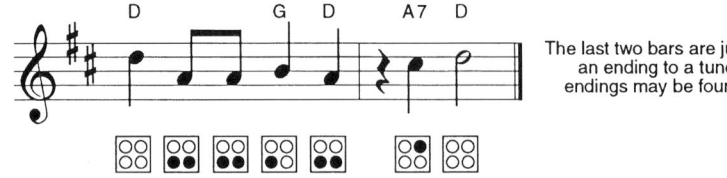

The last two bars are just a suggestion for adding an ending to a tune. More ideas for such endings may be found in book 3 on page 32.

The 'Floral dance' comes from Helston in Cornwall. This old processional dance takes place throughout the town in early May as part of celebrations to welcome the Spring.

Shepherd's hey

English

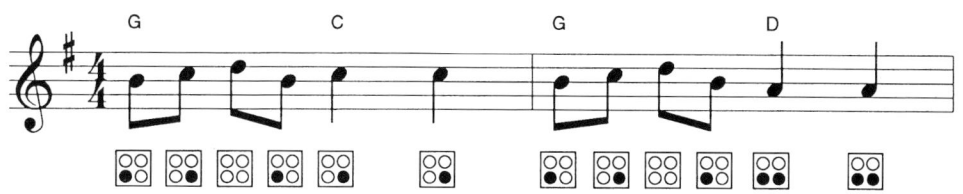

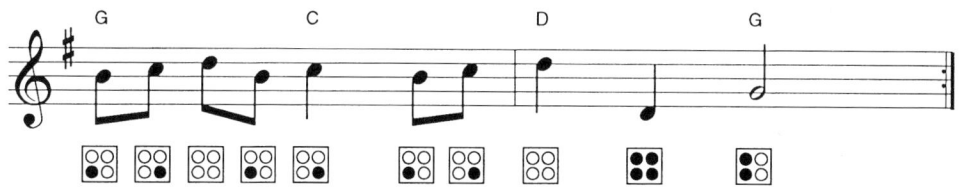

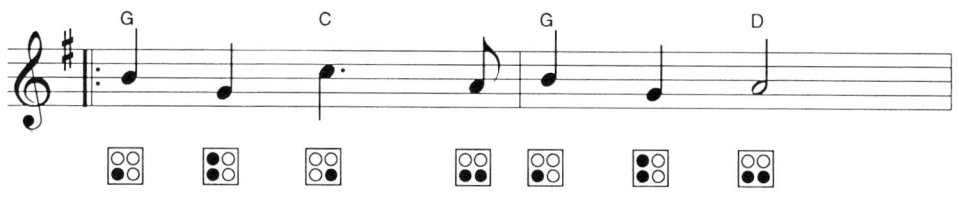

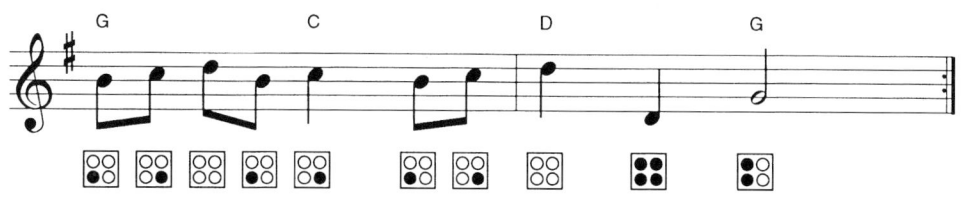

A 'hey' is an English dance dating back as far as the 16th century. As with the Cornish 'Floral dance', the tune is now played for Morris dancing in rural England.

book 2   arrangement copyright © 1992 Ocarina Workshop Publications - copying prohibited   **15**

Can Can
Offenbach

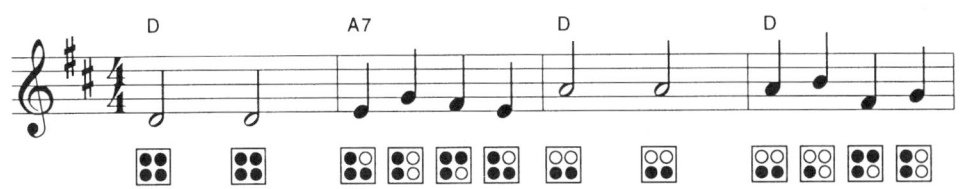
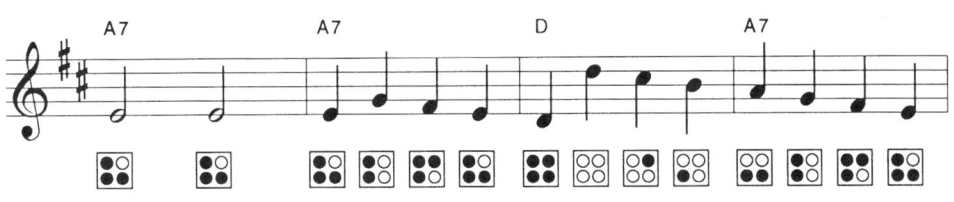
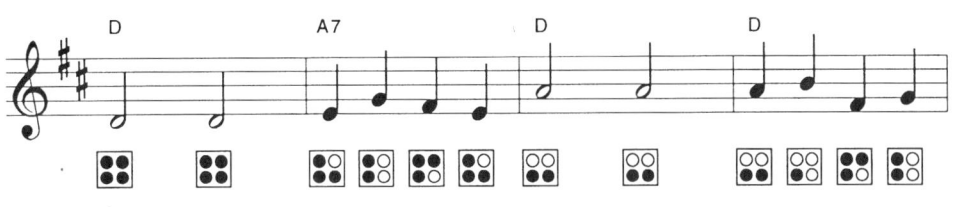
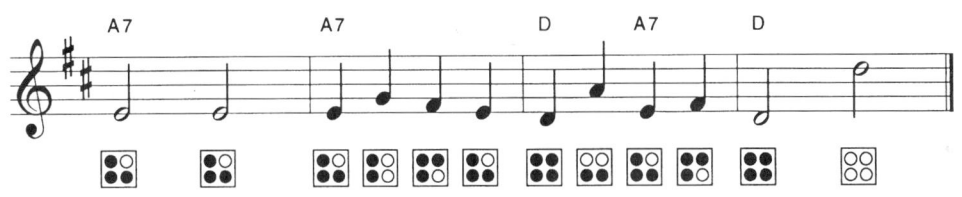

Practise slowly and keep fingers relaxed. When you feel 'easy' with the tune, speed up your performance with precise tonguing, dancing as you play!

Wedding marches

Wagner
Mendelssohn

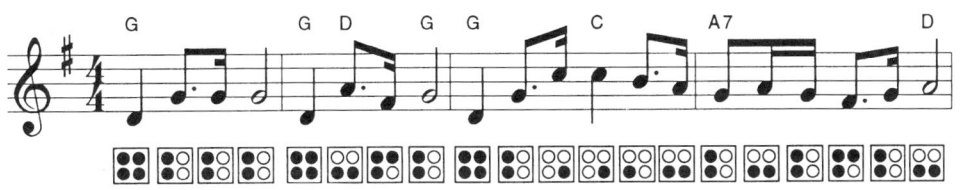
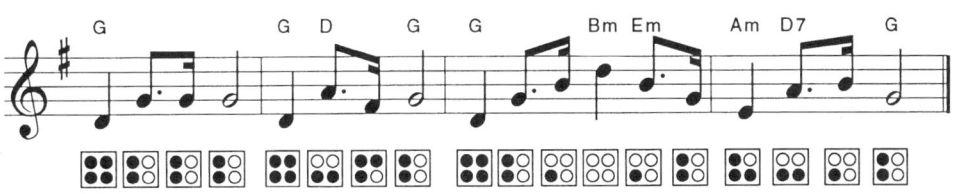
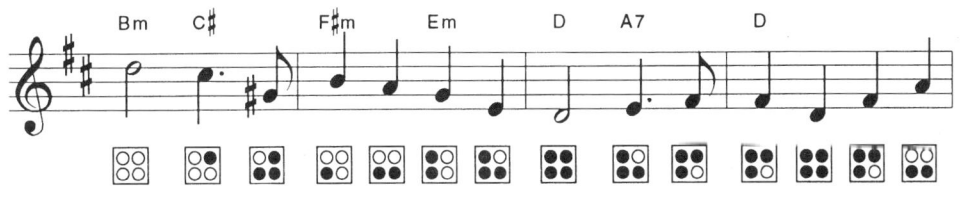
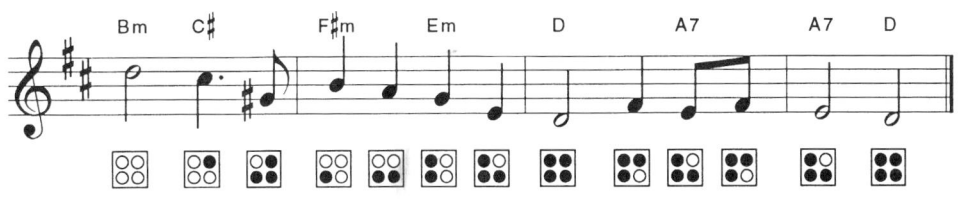

German composers Richard Wagner (1813-1883) and Felix Mendelssohn (1809-1847) were both inspired to write wedding marches that are still frequently heard today.

book 2   arrangement copyright © 1992 Ocarina Workshop Publications - copying prohibited

Group and part playing

Most groups begin with unison playing on alto 'D' ocarinas. It is possible to play rounds very effectively in 2, 3 or 4 parts with ocarinas of the same size or pitch. Some Langley ocarinas are made as 'G' instruments (soprano, tenor, great bass) and these are best avoided in the early stages unless everyone in the group plays them.

In the 'D' range, the bass ocarina plays an octave lower than the alto and, as its name implies, adds a deep and sonorous voice to the group. The mini, by contrast, is an octave higher than the alto, with a distinctive penetrating tone. It should be used sparingly to highlight the climax of a piece or add a descant to the final verse or chorus of a song. The advantage of adding bass or mini ocarinas is that they may be played in unison within a group and yet give the impression of harmony playing because of the combination of different tones. Start simply by playing the tunes and rounds on the following pages. Book 3 contains further materials for solo and group playing.

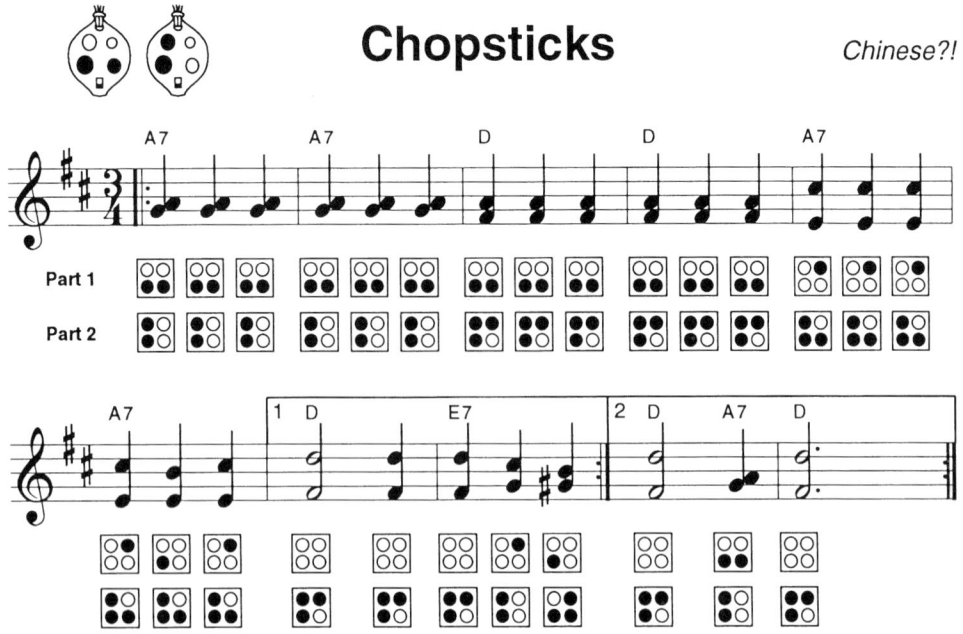

Chopsticks — *Chinese?!*

The cuckoo

3 part round

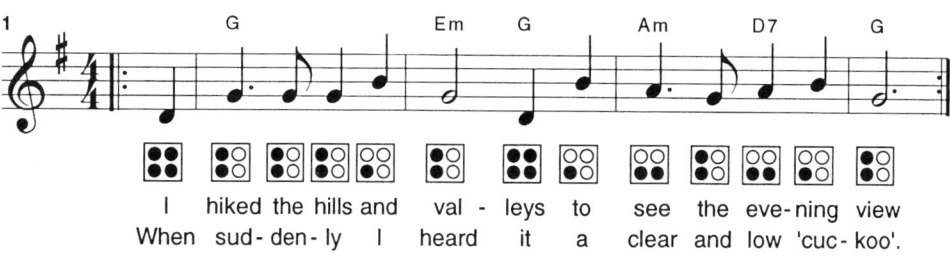

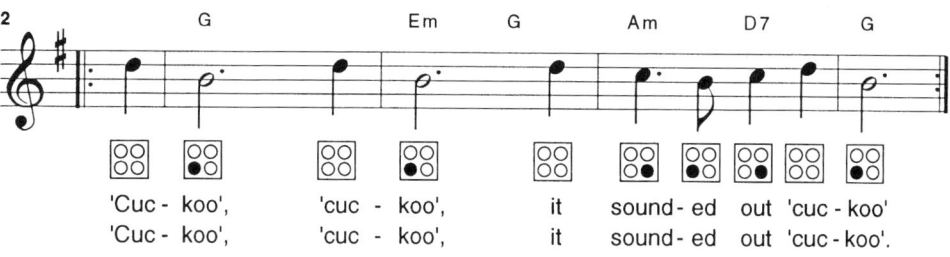

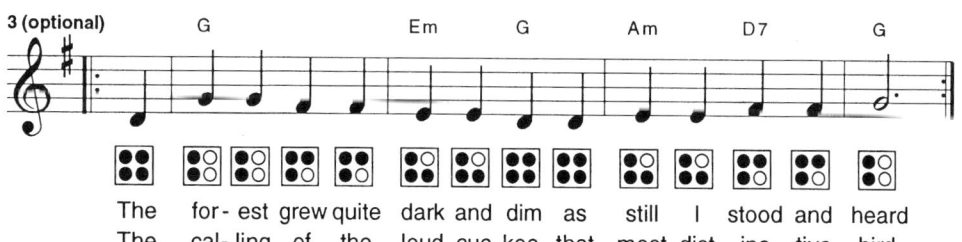

'The cuckoo' can be played in up to 3 parts as a round. Play or sing in unison first. Then each player should come in at the beginning in turn so that parts 1, 2 and 3 are eventually heard simultaneously. Lines 1 and 2 are effective when played on just two ocarinas together. Add the optional third part whenever you can.

In 'Chopsticks' opposite, parts 1 and 2 are played at the same time. Part 1 is always the higher note on the stave. Play the first time bar (marked 1) only on your first time through and play the second time bar in its place at the end of the repeat.

Sing a little song

4 part round

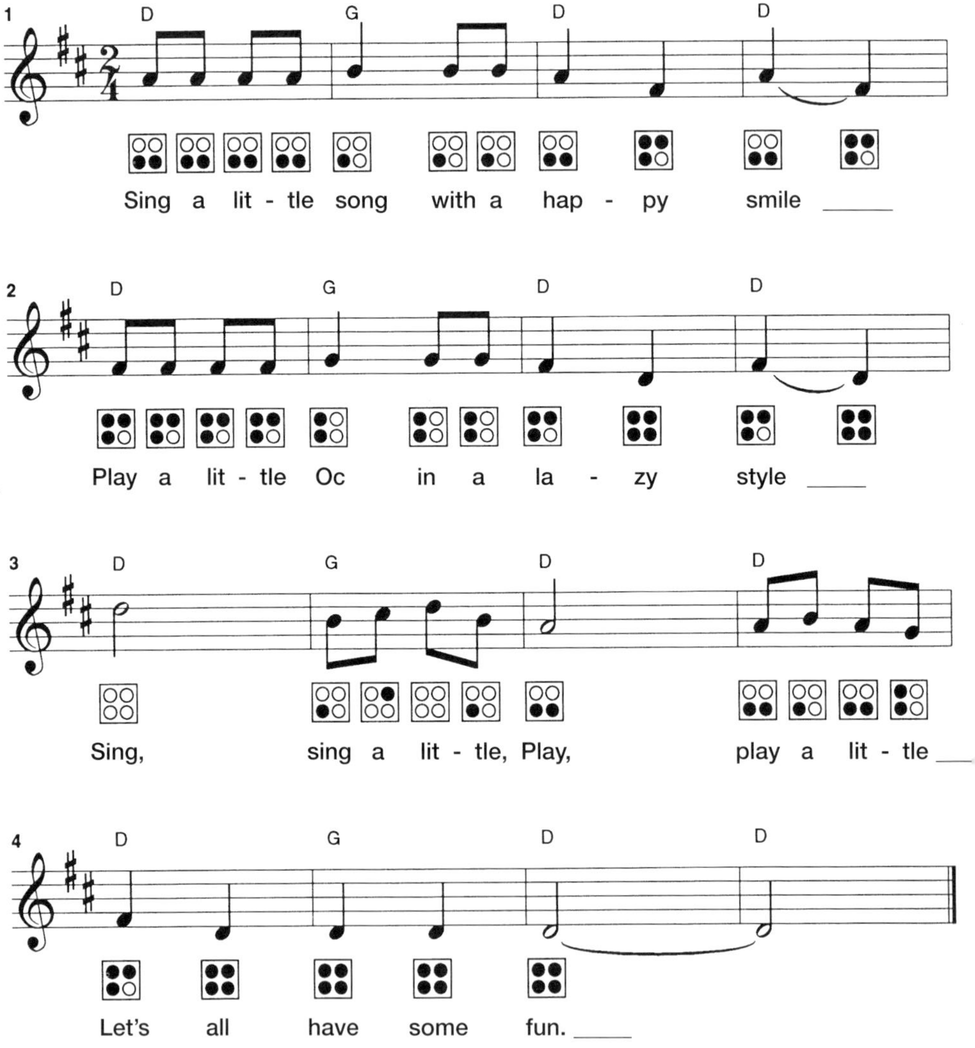
1
D G D D
Sing a lit - tle song with a hap - py smile
2
D G D D
Play a lit - tle Oc in a la - zy style
3
D G D D
Sing, sing a lit - tle, Play, play a lit - tle
4
D G D D
Let's all have some fun.

Both these rounds can be played in up to 4 parts. It is also possible to split parts for 'Tallis' canon' after every 4 notes instead of every line (follow numbers in brackets).

Tallis' canon

4 part round

1 (1) G | C | D7 | G | **(2)** | Am | D7 | G
Glor - y | to | thee | my | God | this | night
Praise | God, | from | whom | all | bles - sings | flow;

2 (3) G | C | D7 | G | **(4)** | Am | D7 | G
For | all | the | bles - sings | of | the | light;
Praise | him, | all | crea - tures | here | be - low;

3 G | C | D7 | G | Am | D7 | G
Keep | me, | O | keep | me, | King | of | kings,
Praise | him | a - bove, | ye | heaven - ly | host;

4 G | C | D7 | G | Am | D7 | G
Be - neath | thine | own | al - migh - ty | wings.
Praise | Fa - ther, | Son | and | Ho - ly | Ghost.

Thomas Tallis (1505-1585) wrote this well known tune around the year 1567. Words were added in 1692 by Bishop Ken and the first and last verses appear above.

Muss i'denn

German

See page 24 for instructions on playing this note

book 2

Elvis Presley recorded 'Muss i'denn' in 1960 under the title 'Wooden Heart'. He sang it in the film 'G.I.Blues' and over a million copies of the record were sold in Europe alone.

book 2   **23**

Nose-shading

Play the pattern of notes below. Every time you see the sign ⛉ play a low 'D' and tilt the string-end of the ocarina upwards. This lowers the pitch by a semitone to a low 'C#'.

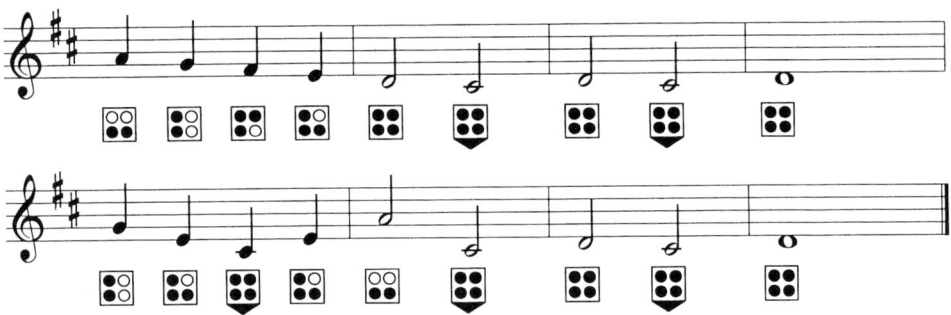

This technique is called 'nose-shading'. Try to accurately pitch the low 'C#'. Tilt the ocarina with a clear definite movement to give precise tuning.

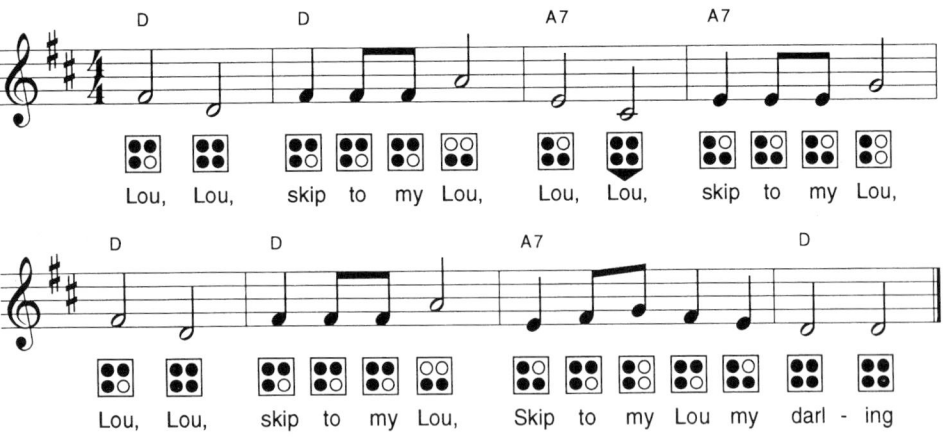

It is possible to bend notes by more than a semitone. Some players can nose-shade down as far as low 'B' or even 'A', particularly on small ocarinas. On larger ocarinas it is easier to 'lip-shade' notes rather than 'nose-shade'. Push the mouthpiece further into your mouth so that your top lip moves closer to the whistle-hole.

Mastering these techniques will extend the range of your playing. The ability to bend notes subtly is particularly useful when playing in a 'Blues' style.

National anthem

British
American

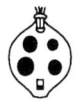

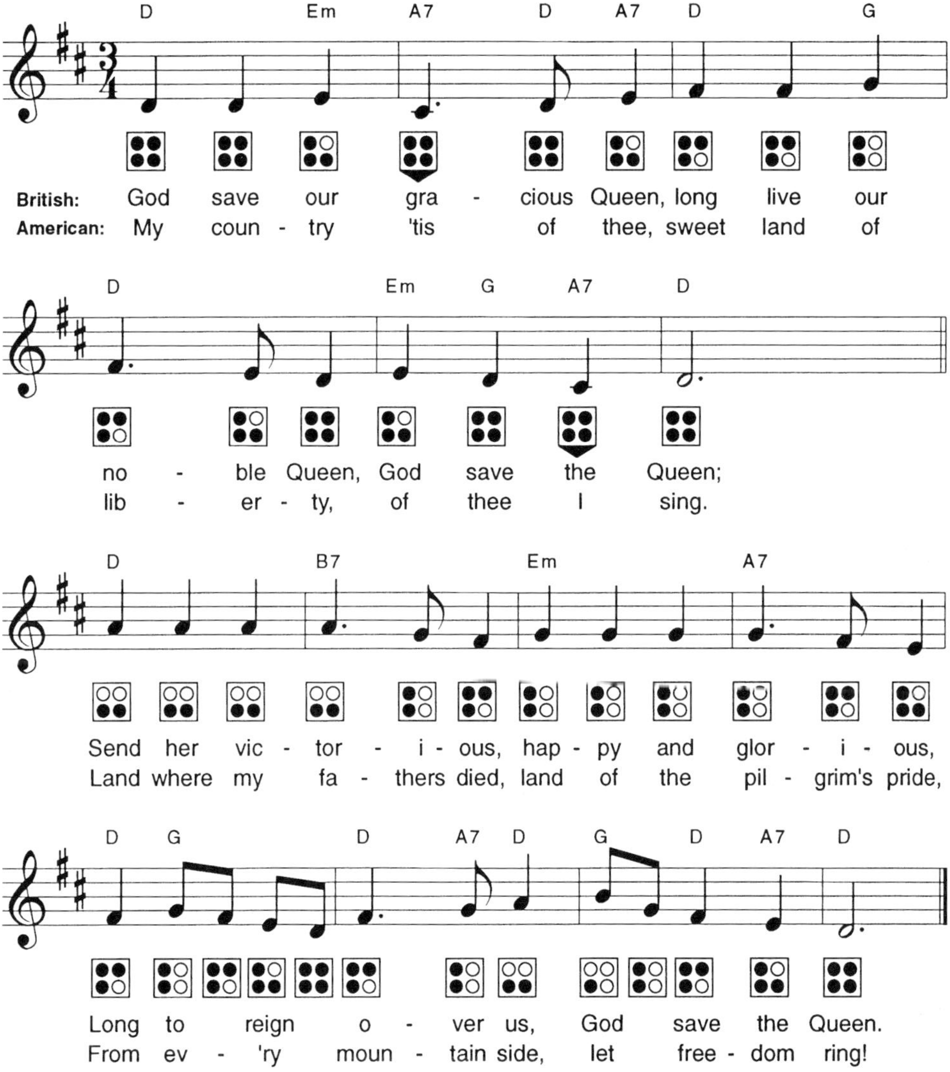

The tune to the British national anthem appeared in print in 1744 and has been used since by many different countries. British and American versions are shown above.

Thumb-holes

It is possible to play extra notes using the thumb-holes of a 6-hole ocarina. Top 'E' is particularly useful and can be played by opening all holes. It is important to support the ocarina at the string-end with third and fourth fingers so that the ocarina feels secure when all the holes are open.

6-hole ocarinas are tuned so that top 'D' sounds best with the small left thumb-hole open. For well-tuned performance always play top 'D' like this on the 6-hole ocarina. Practise the beginnings of 'Twinkle twinkle' and 'Kumbaya' below to explore these new finger and thumb combinations.

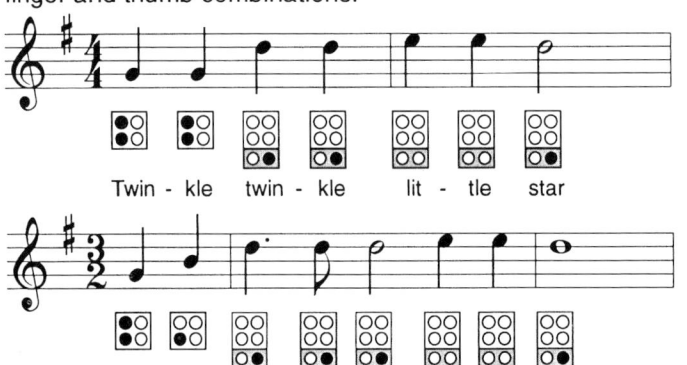

In these tunes a finger-chart reminds you to lift your left thumb to play top 'D'. However in all other tunes you have to remember this for yourself as just the 4-hole chart appears.

Breath control is important for making a good sound on top notes. Squeaks can occur if you blow too strongly or weakly or in an uncontrolled way.

As well as tuning top 'D', the small thumb-hole allows accurate playing of low 'D#' and 'F'. These notes are introduced on page 28. High 'D#' can also be played on the 6-hole ocarina, completing a fully chromatic range of 16 notes. All fingerings are illustrated inside the back cover. Tunes in books 3 and 4 make use of all these notes. Try the extract below which is the opening of 'The Entertainer' from book 4 and see if you can work out how to play low and high 'D#'.

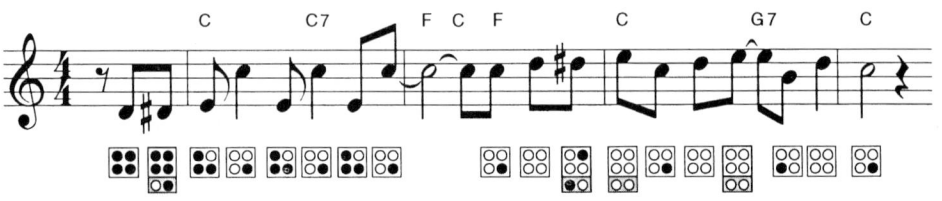

26 book 2

Auld lang syne

Scottish

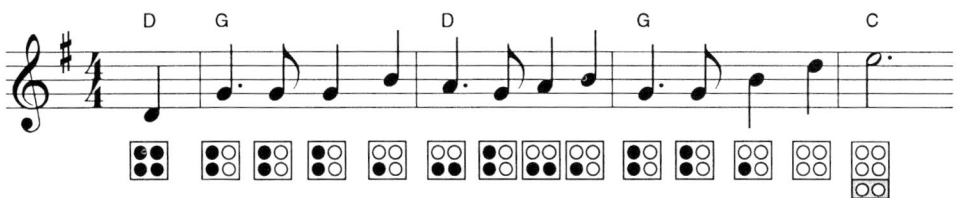

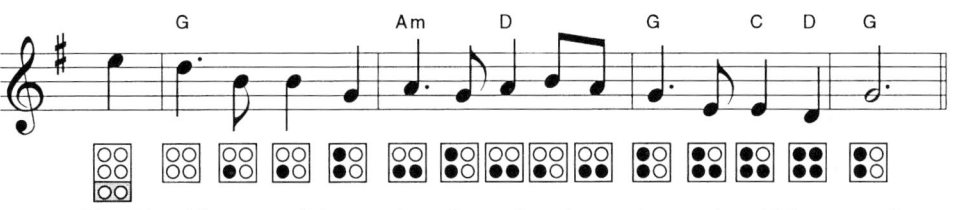

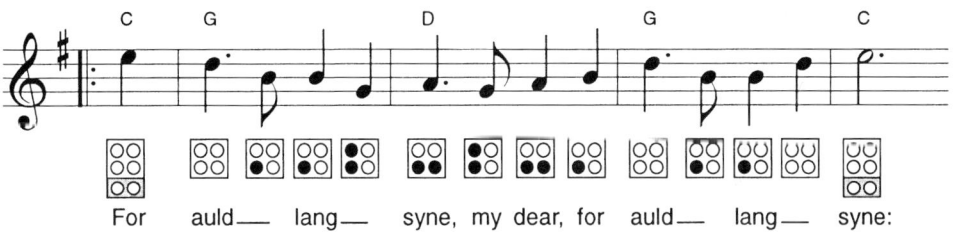

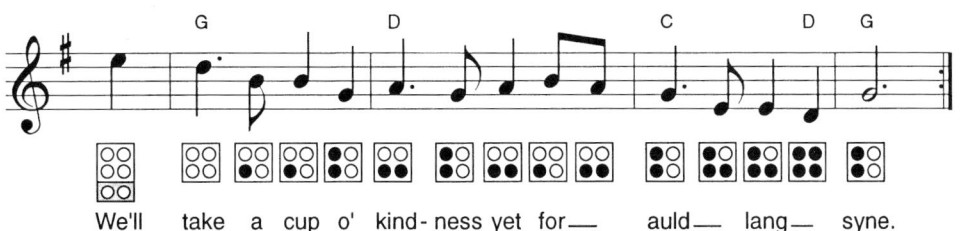

This traditional tune with words by Robert Burns is sung all over the world and especially when celebrating the arrival of New Year.

Semitones

It is possible to half-cover holes when playing 'E' or 'F#' to **lower** the pitch of these notes by a semitone. This changes 'E' to 'D#' and 'F#' to 'F natural'. This is the simplest way to play 'D#' and 'F' on both 4-hole and 6-hole ocarinas although skill is required in tuning the notes accurately.

On the 6-hole ocarina, these notes ('D#' and 'F') can also be produced by playing a note lower ('D' and 'E') and by opening the small left thumb-hole to **raise** the pitch a semitone. This gives greater ease of tuning but is not so easy when playing quickly or trilling.

These two methods of playing 'D#' and 'F' both appear in the charts of the tunes below and opposite. They also appear in the reference section inside the back cover. Only the 6-hole version is normally given so it is worth remembering and practising the alternative fingerings for occasions when they may be more appropriately chosen.

Black eyes — *Russian*

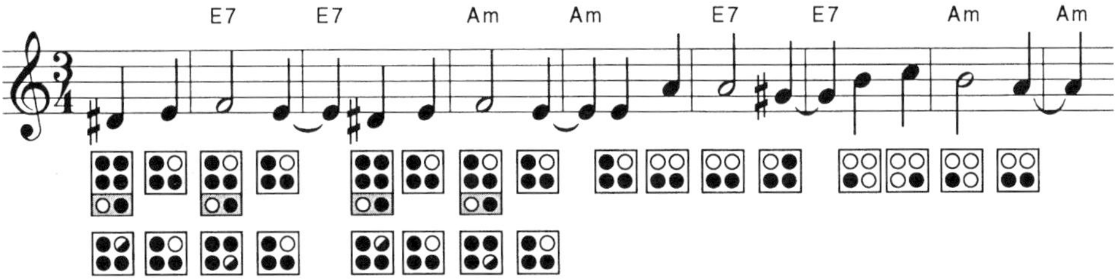

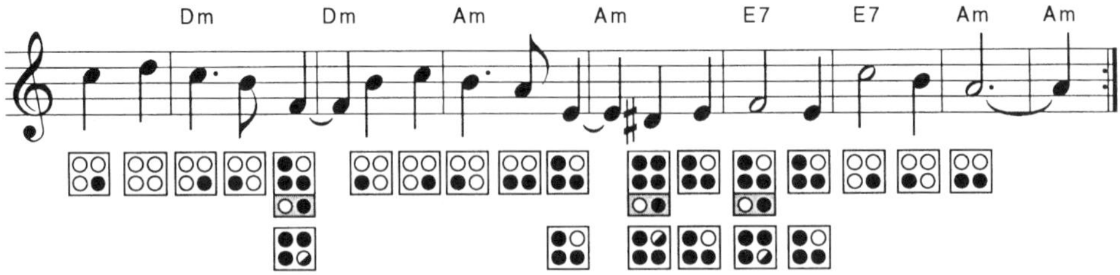

Spring song

Mendelssohn

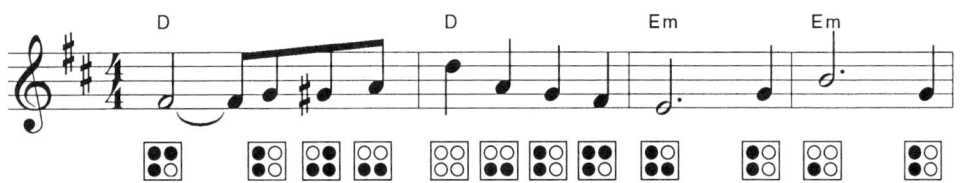
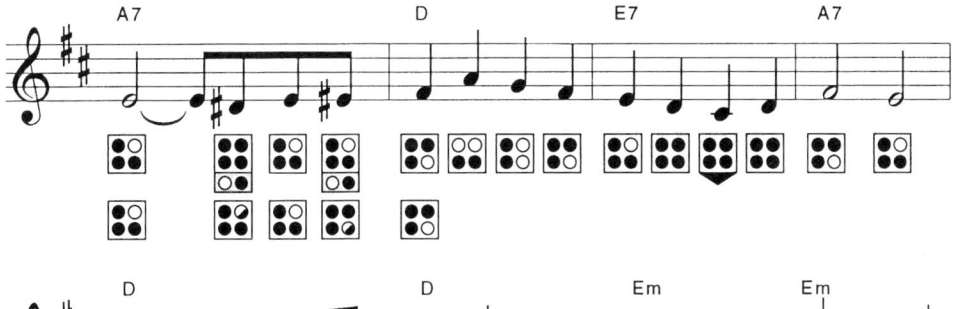
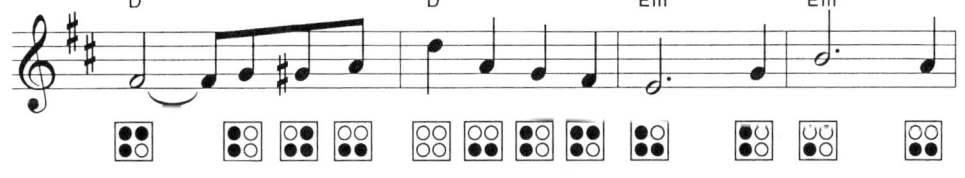
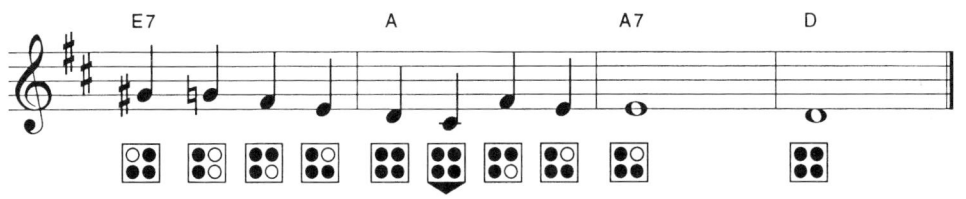

The note E# in the 5th bar is the same as F natural. See book 1 page 22 for a description of how notes are named.

book 2 — arrangement copyright © 1992 Ocarina Workshop Publications - copying prohibited — 29

My grandfather's clock
American

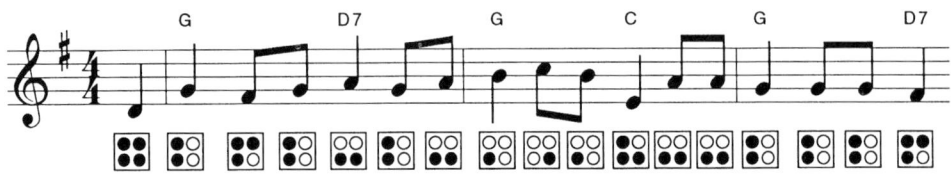

1. My grand-fa-ther's clock was too tall for the shelf so it stood nine-ty years
2. In watch-ing its pen-du-lum swing to and fro ma-ny hours had he spent
3. My grand-fa-ther said that of those he could hire not a ser-vant so faith-

on the floor. It was tall-er by far than the old man him-self,
while a boy. And in child-hood and man-hood the clock seemed to know
ful he found, for it wast-ed no time and had but one de-sire

tho' it weighed not a pen-ny-weight more. It was bought on the morn
and to share both his trou-ble and joy. For it struck twen-ty- four
at the end of each week to be wound. And it kept in its place,

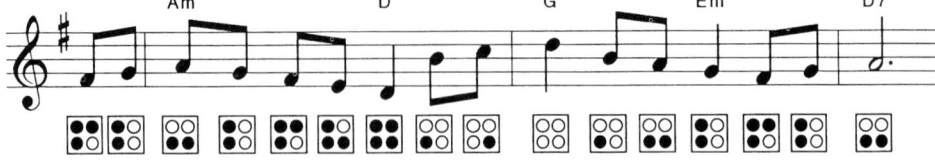

of the day that he was born and was al-ways his plea-sure and pride,
when he op-ened up the door with a bloom-ing and beau-ti-ful bride,
not a frown up-on its face, and its hands nev-er hung by its side,

Henry Clay Work (1832-1884) was an American writer of popular songs. This song was written in 1876 and other songs included 'Marching through Georgia'.

For he's a jolly good fellow

Sing and play this whenever you have cause to congratulate someone. Change 'he' to 'she' as often as you like. You can also sing 'they are' and 'fellows' for group efforts!

32   arrangement copyright © 1992 Ocarina Workshop Publications - copying prohibited   book 2